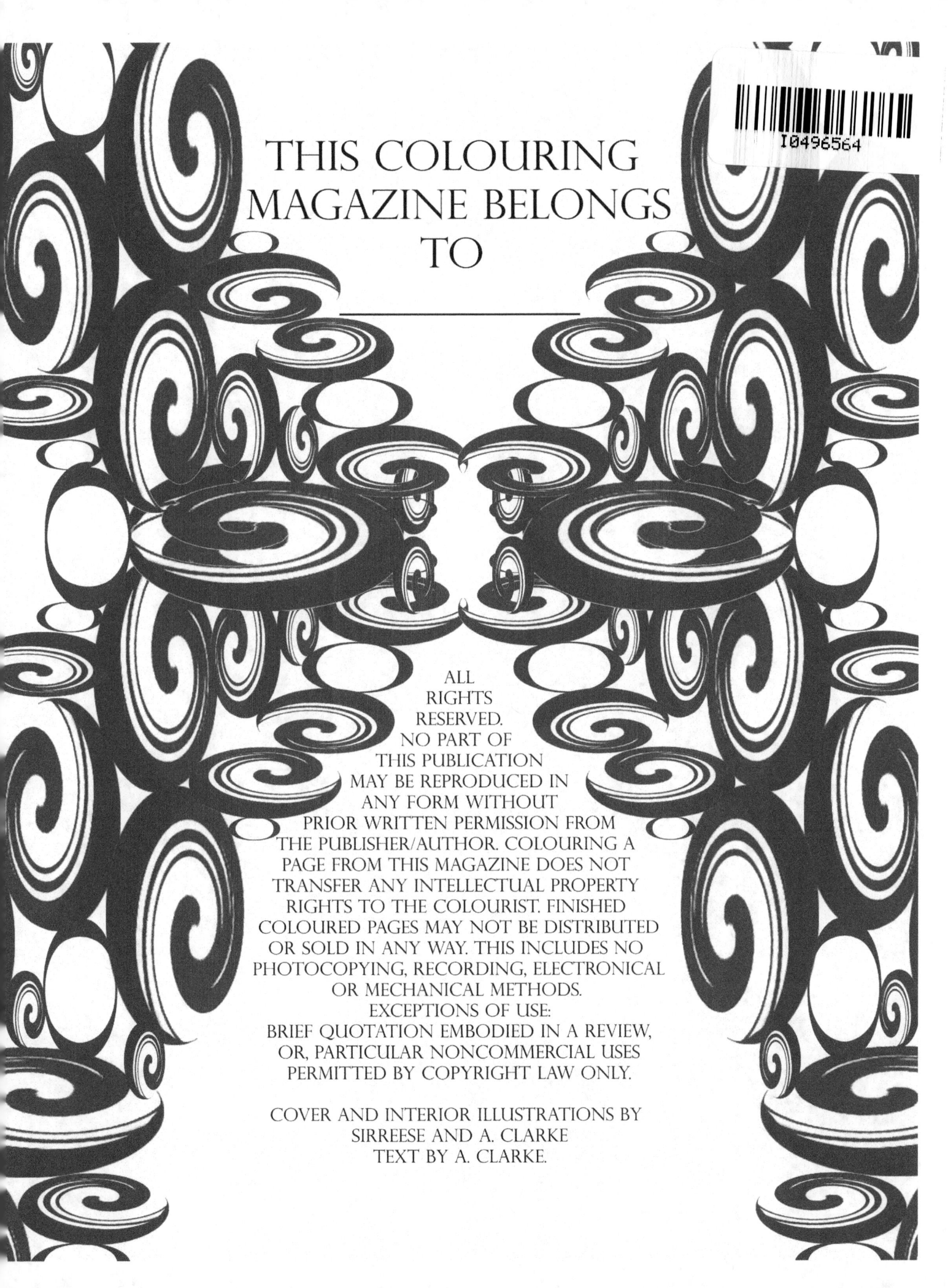

THIS COLOURING MAGAZINE BELONGS TO
_____

ALL RIGHTS RESERVED. NO PART OF THIS PUBLICATION MAY BE REPRODUCED IN ANY FORM WITHOUT PRIOR WRITTEN PERMISSION FROM THE PUBLISHER/AUTHOR. COLOURING A PAGE FROM THIS MAGAZINE DOES NOT TRANSFER ANY INTELLECTUAL PROPERTY RIGHTS TO THE COLOURIST. FINISHED COLOURED PAGES MAY NOT BE DISTRIBUTED OR SOLD IN ANY WAY. THIS INCLUDES NO PHOTOCOPYING, RECORDING, ELECTRONICAL OR MECHANICAL METHODS.
EXCEPTIONS OF USE:
BRIEF QUOTATION EMBODIED IN A REVIEW, OR, PARTICULAR NONCOMMERCIAL USES PERMITTED BY COPYRIGHT LAW ONLY.

COVER AND INTERIOR ILLUSTRATIONS BY SIRREESE AND A. CLARKE
TEXT BY A. CLARKE.

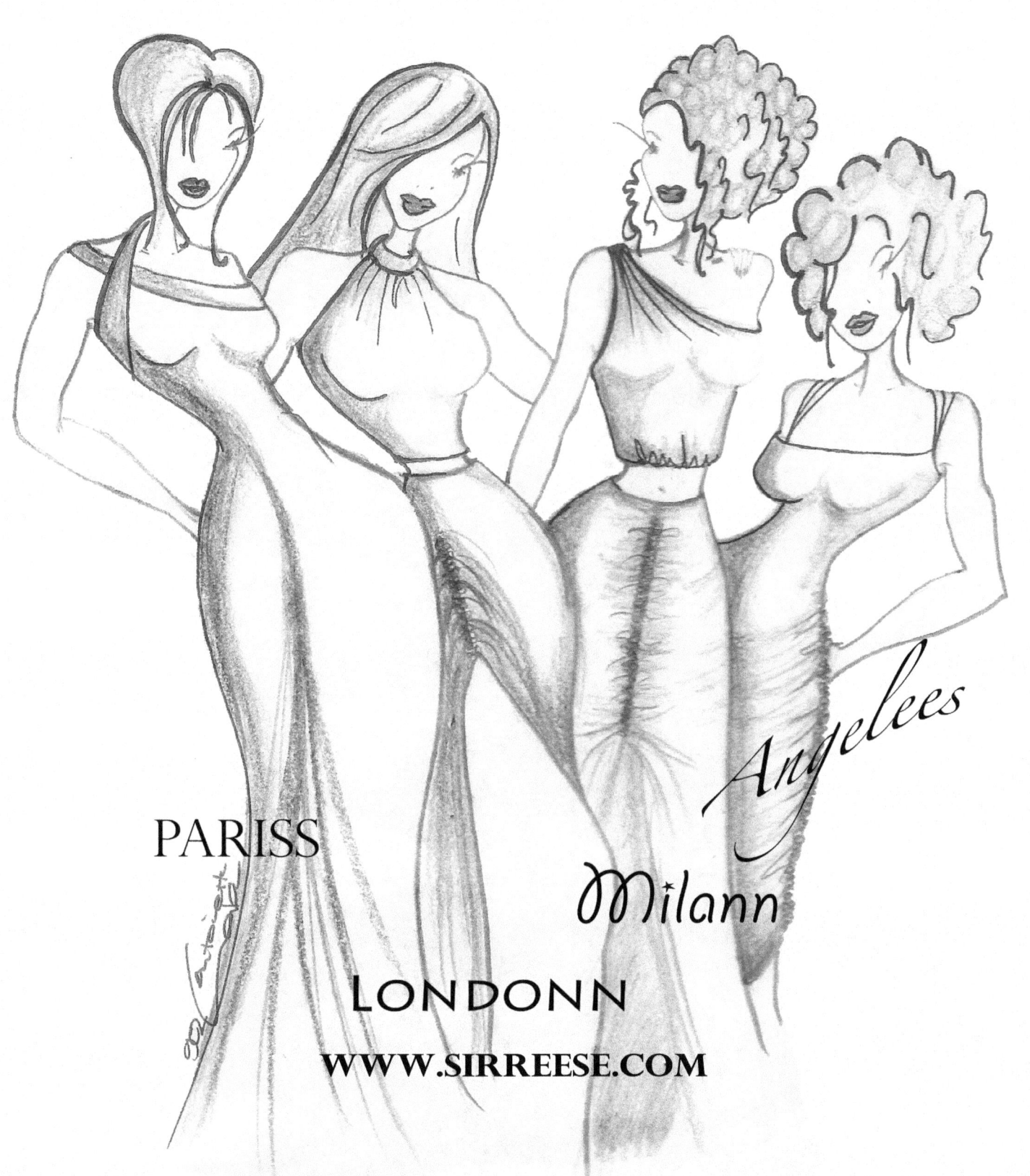

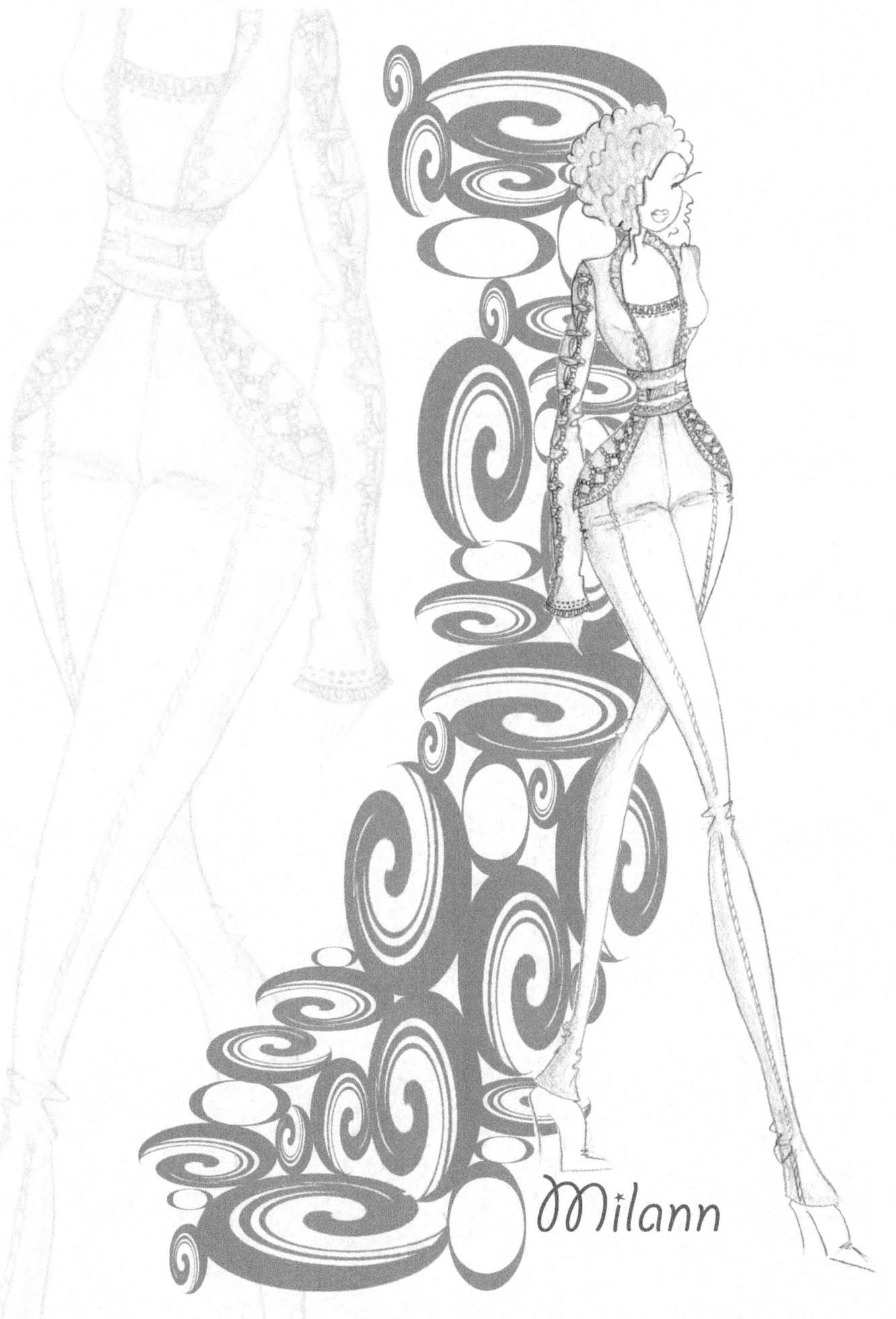

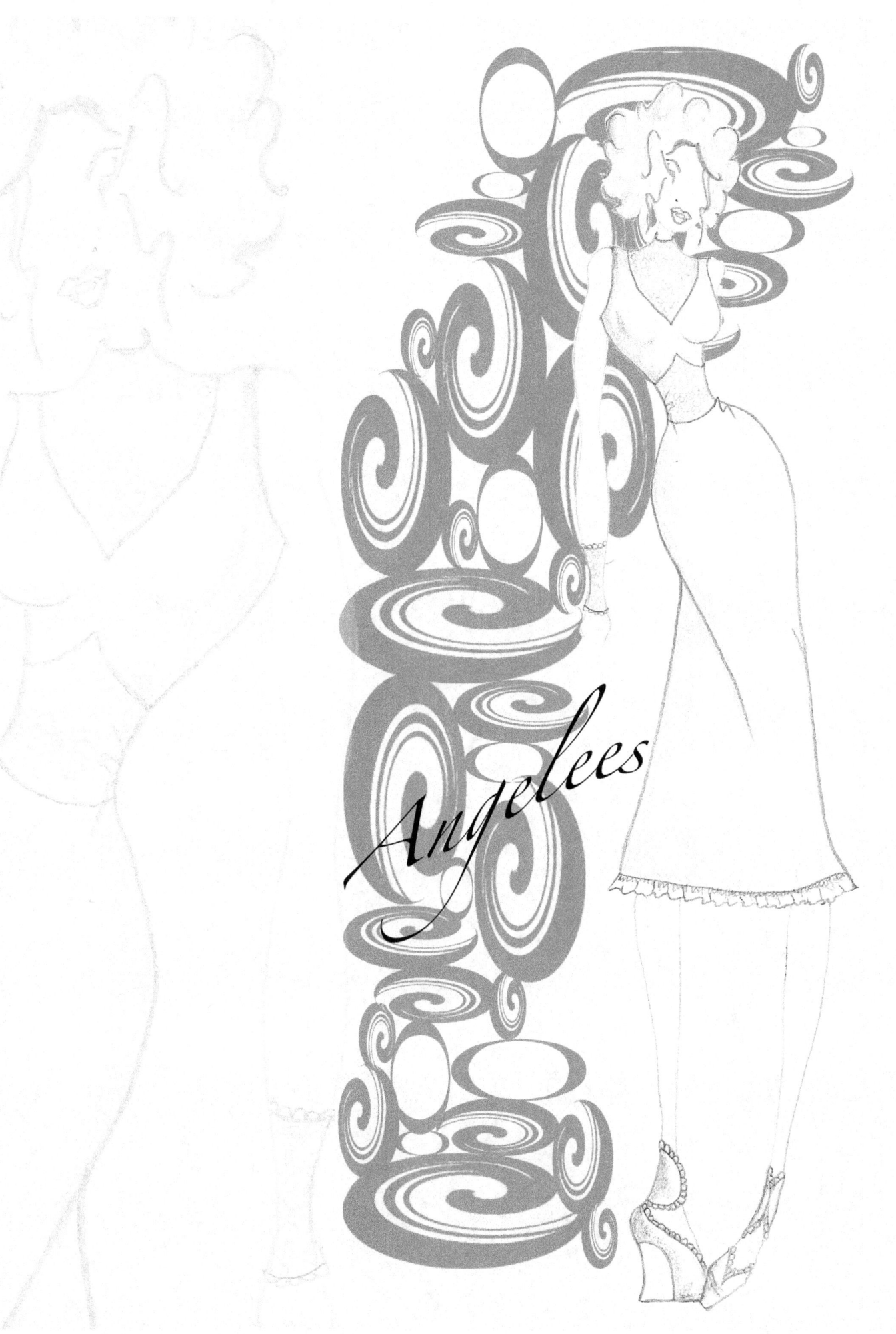

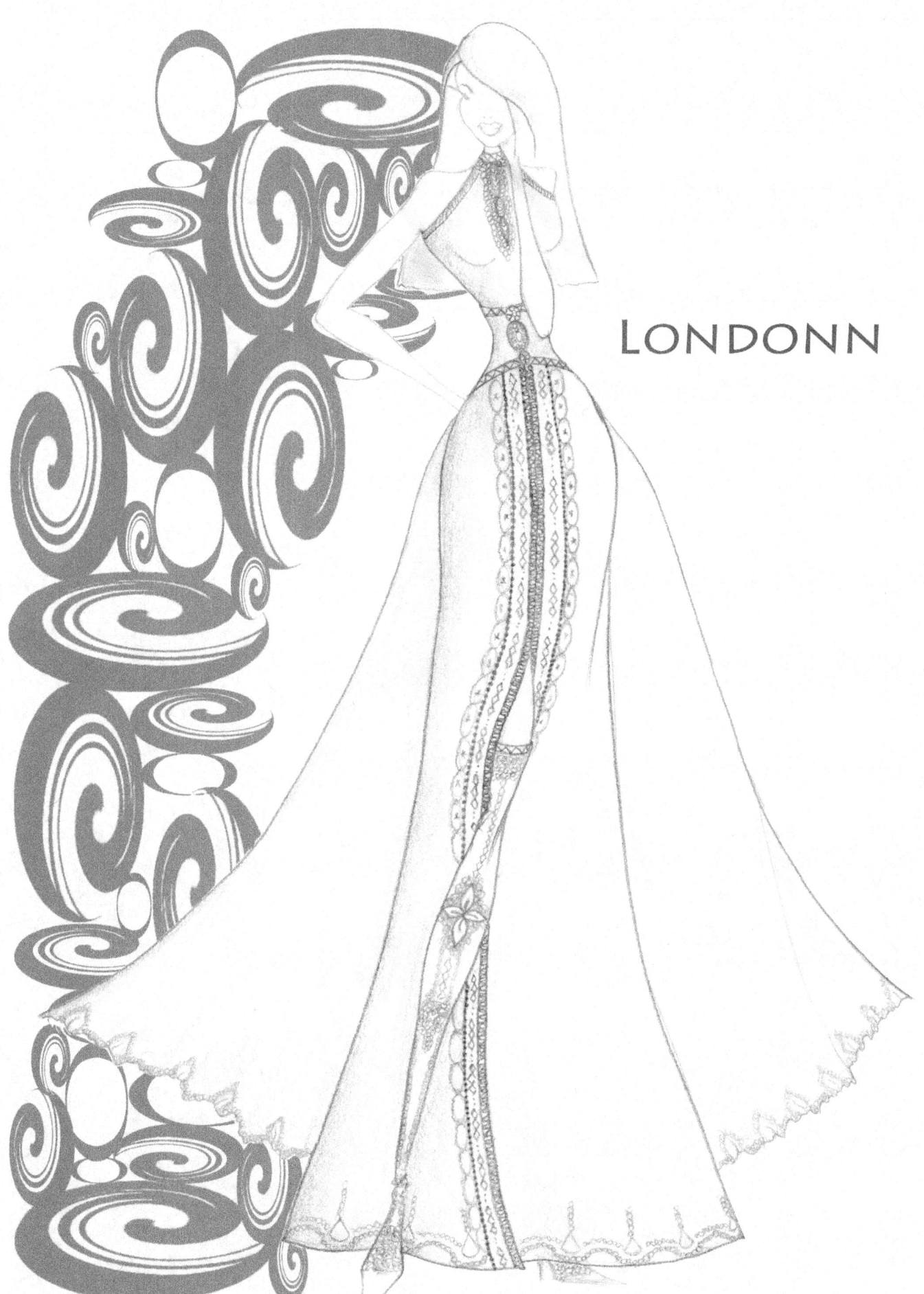

LONDONN

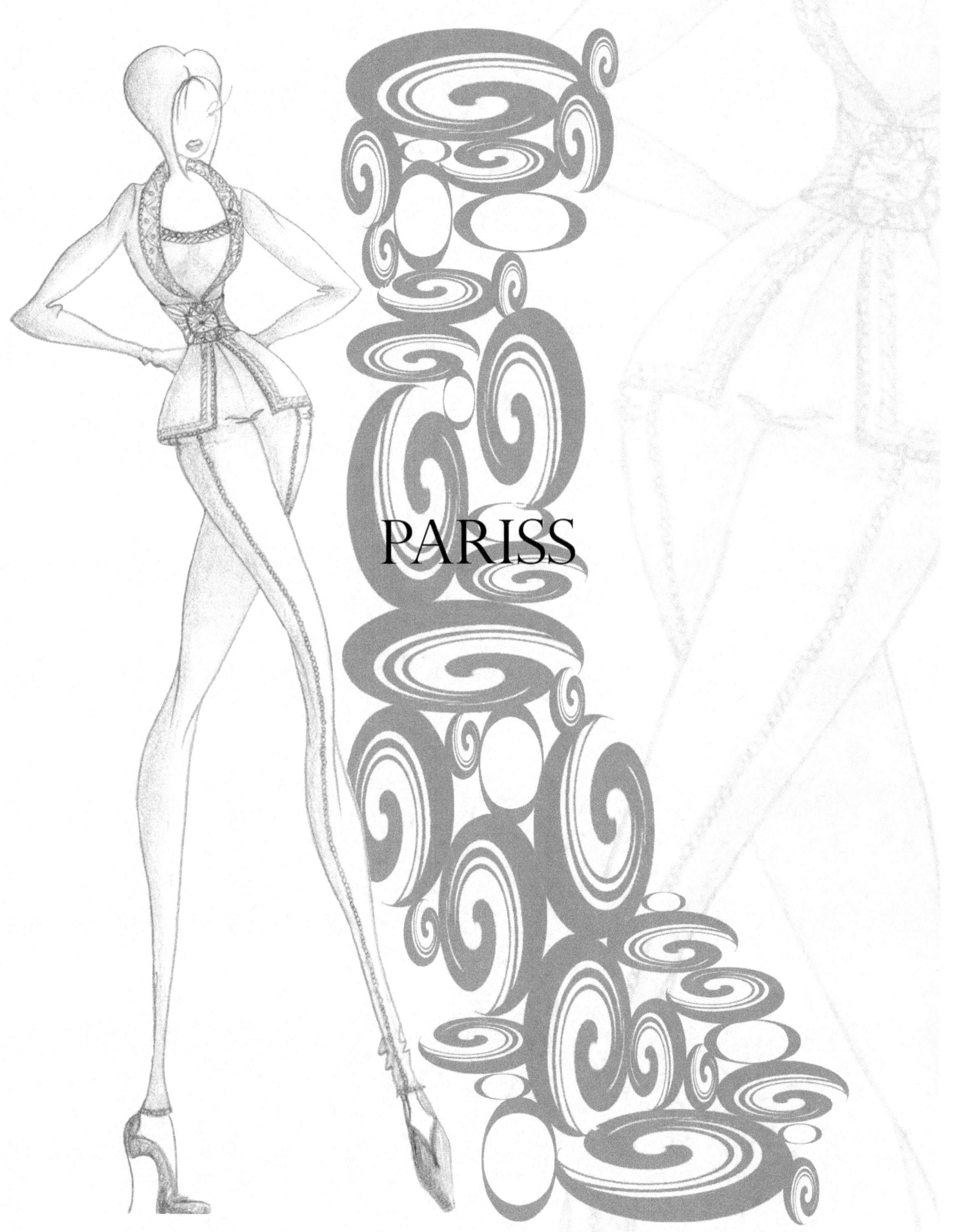

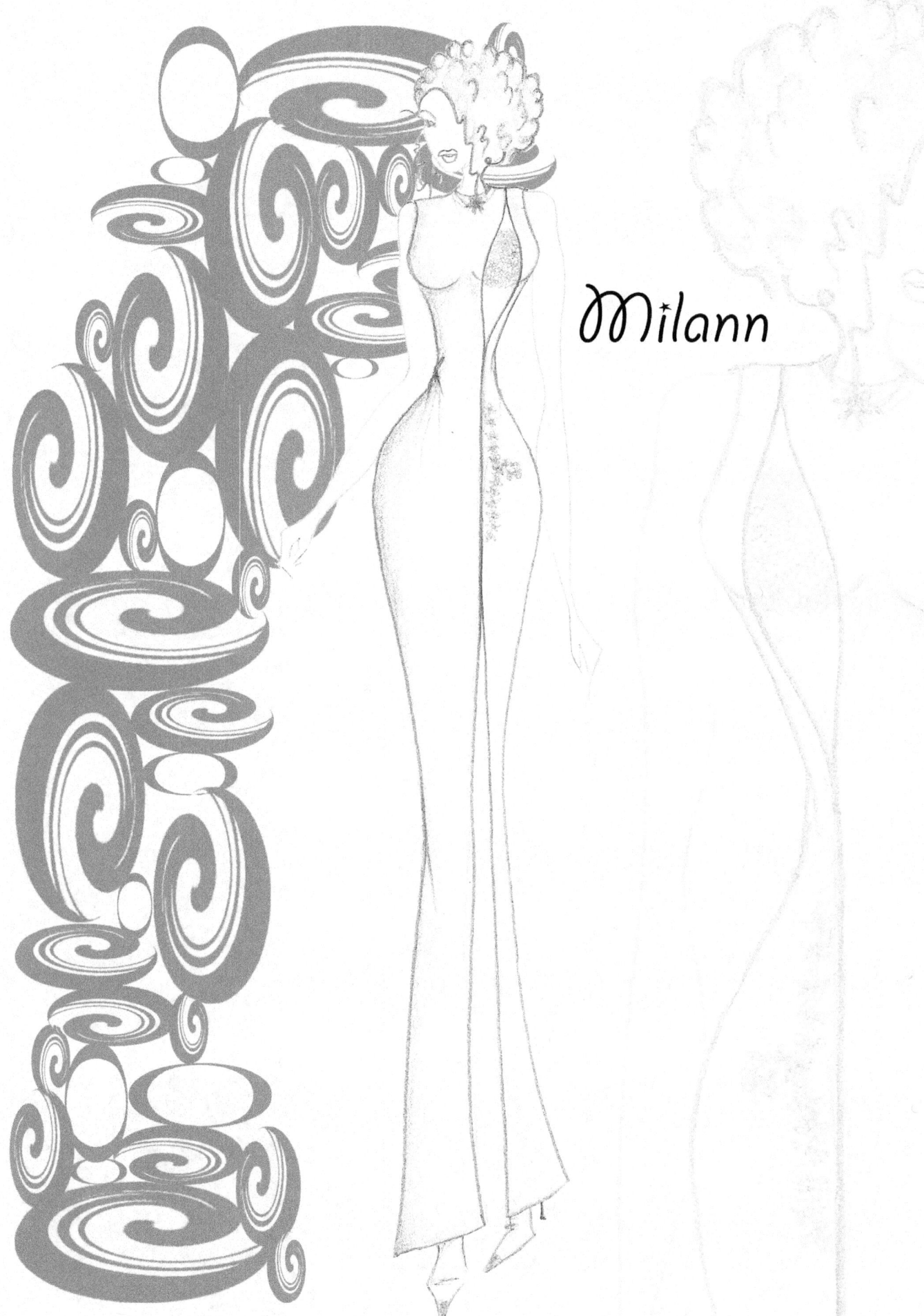

Milann

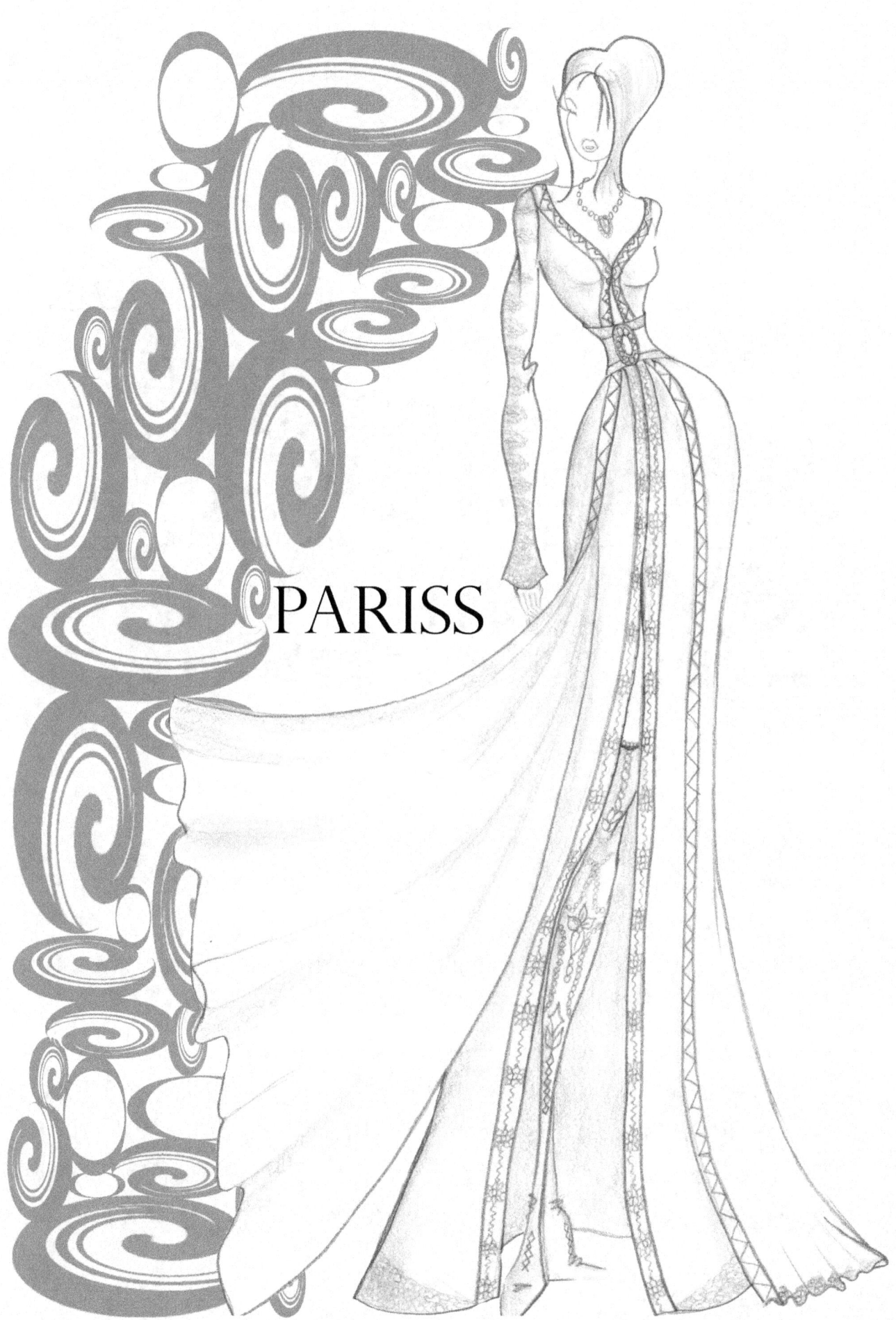

PARISS

Blue City

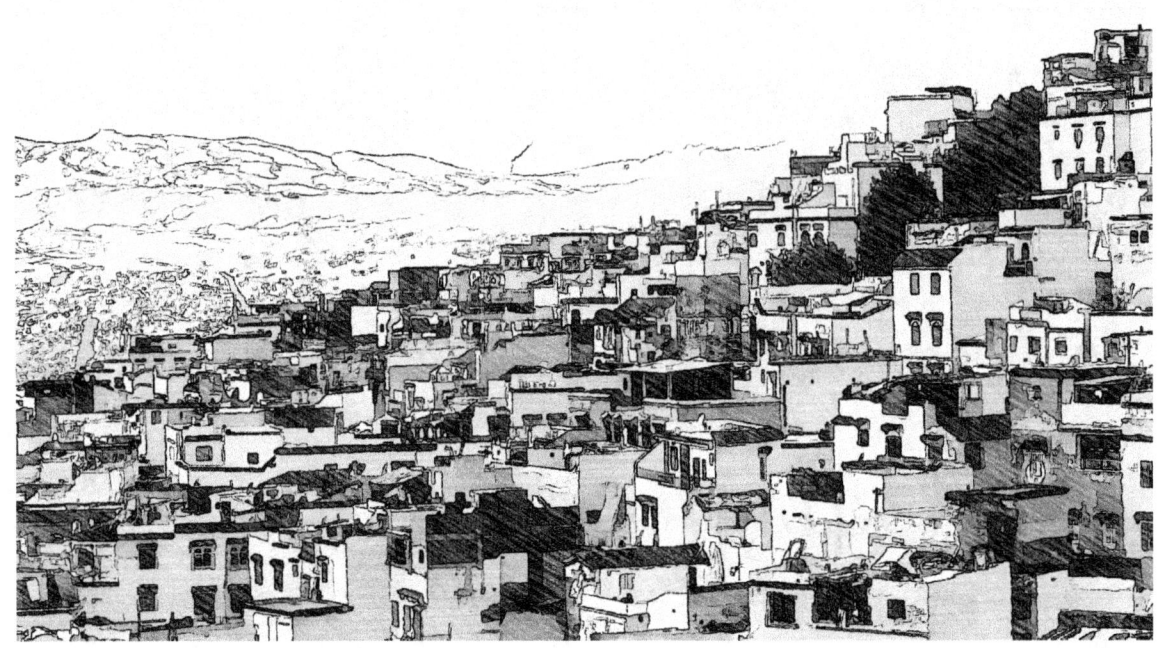

Surrounded on all sides by mountains, Chefchaouen was founded in 1471 with a fortress in the middle, built to help defend attacks from the Portuguese as Portugal was attacking the northern cities and towns of Morocco at the time. Eventually a settlement evolved outside of the fortress by Moors from Spain, local tribes, large numbers of Jewish refugees fleeing from the Spanish Inquisition and later Jews fleeing from Hitler in the Second World War, but many later left to live in Israel. It's said that they introduced the tradition of painting the walls of the buildings blue in keeping with their cultural and religious practices. Not just the houses were painted blue, but also Government buildings, public squares, Mosques, lampposts and even the rubbish bins are all painted blue…everything! In the Islamic culture, the colour blue is said to be a colour of happiness. Some say that the blue walls help to keep the houses cool in warmer months and others say the blue shades helps to keep the mosquitoes away. A good reason as to why the tradition is kept in modern times.

KHIZANAT AL QARAWIYYIN

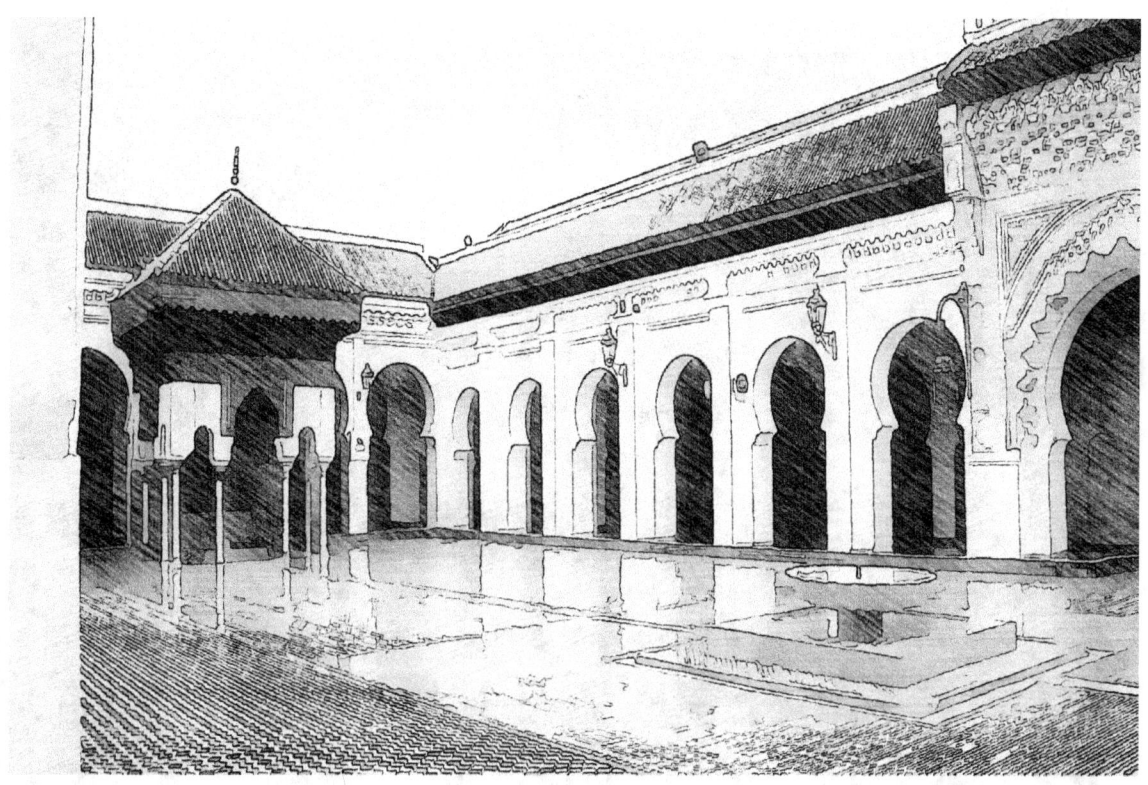

The Library/University of Al Qarawiyyin in Fez, Morocco, Africa, the oldest in the world, opened its doors in 859 and was founded by Fatima Al-Fihri. The restored library has a collection of over 4,000 rare books and ancient Arabic manuscripts, some of which are wrapped up to prevent them from disintegrating in your hands and under strict security has a new underground canal system to drain away the moisture to protect its most prized manuscripts. One of the most precious is a copy of the Qur'an written in ornate Kufic script on camel skin from the 9th century. Many refurbishments have taken place on the library over the years. The recent restoration of the library has equipped it with digital locks to the room with rare books and air conditioning to control the humidity and protect books in the library. This university is well equipped with instruments used in astronomy. The "timers room" is the chamber that accommodates the equipment such as sand clocks, sundials, astrolabes and other instruments for the calculation of time..

Al Quaraoiyine

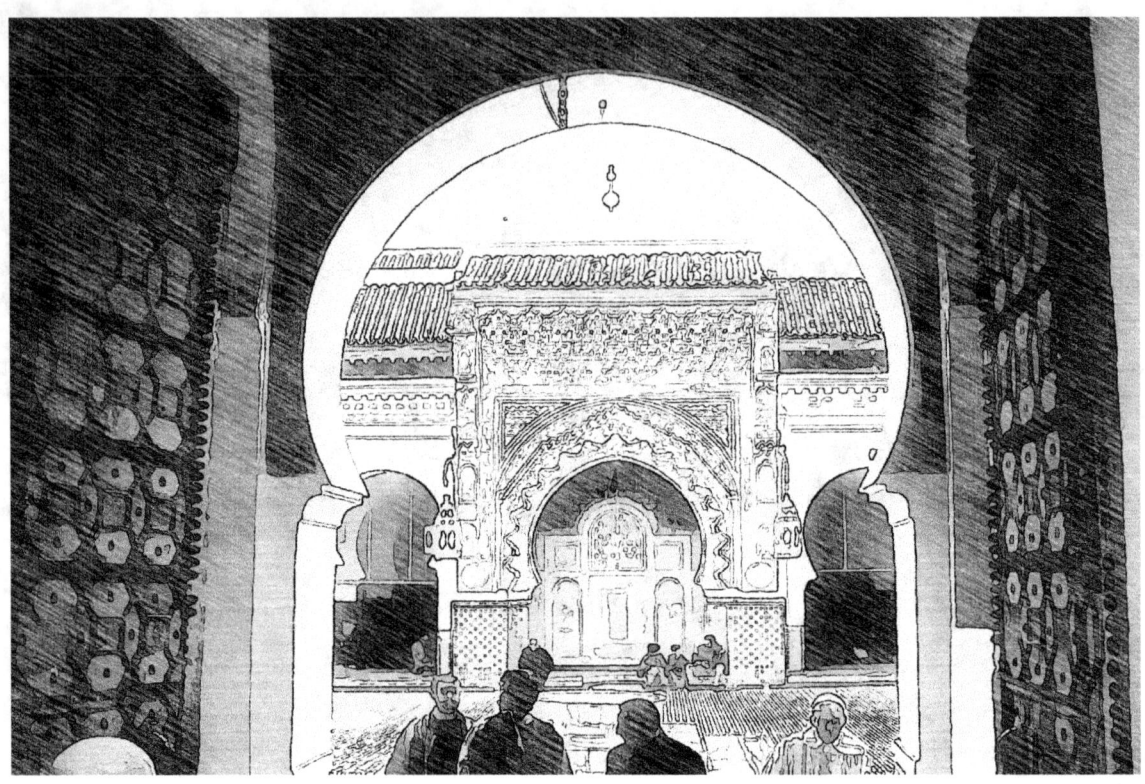

The present form of the mosque is the result of over a 1000 years evolution course. The mosque was originally about 30 meters long with a courtyard located to the west tiled in blue and white with 3 marble fountains and 4 transverse aisles featuring horseshoe arches decorated with beautiful floral Andalusian art, with Kufic Calligraphy around the borders. The first expansion happened in 956, the minaret was relocated and the prayer hall was extended. How the mosque looks today is due to the biggest reconstruction in 1135 extending the mosque's 18 aisles to 21, enlarging the structure to more than 3,000 square meters. 2 pavilions were added to the north and the south ends of the courtyard when the mosque was restored in the 16th century. The kiosks are the most elegant parts of the mosque with slender marble columns

The sections above were sculptured in beautiful golden embroidery displaying exquisite floral and geometrical forms framed with calligraphy. It became tradition that other mosques of Fez would call to prayer only after they heard Al Quaraouiyine.

Word Search

```
              I N
            A G B B
          G Y F G U L
        U M N H R A E U
        U O F E Z B I H Y E
      Q N W Z V K K M C M Y C
      X O I Y Q S U N D I A L S I
    A R L V M E G O P R G R I F A T
    X T A I E G U O F K D Y D U J T H Y
  K S T H B R A L Q U A R A O U I Y I N E
  A O D Q R S Q S V C U G X K J U D F P F
    C C E A I C A L L I G R A P H Y Z Z
    Y Z R T H Y A S T R O L A B E S
      Y Y Y Y P N P Z A B D E L W
        A N C B L R T S V A L E
        H M E L I L L A S O
          U G R Q X P Z X
          H L A M S R
            K I J V
            B W
```

Morocco, Bluecity, Abdelkrim, Africa, Khizanat, Sundials, Fatimaalfihri, Astronomy, Melilla, Fez, Library, Mosque, Calligraphy, University, Astrolabes.

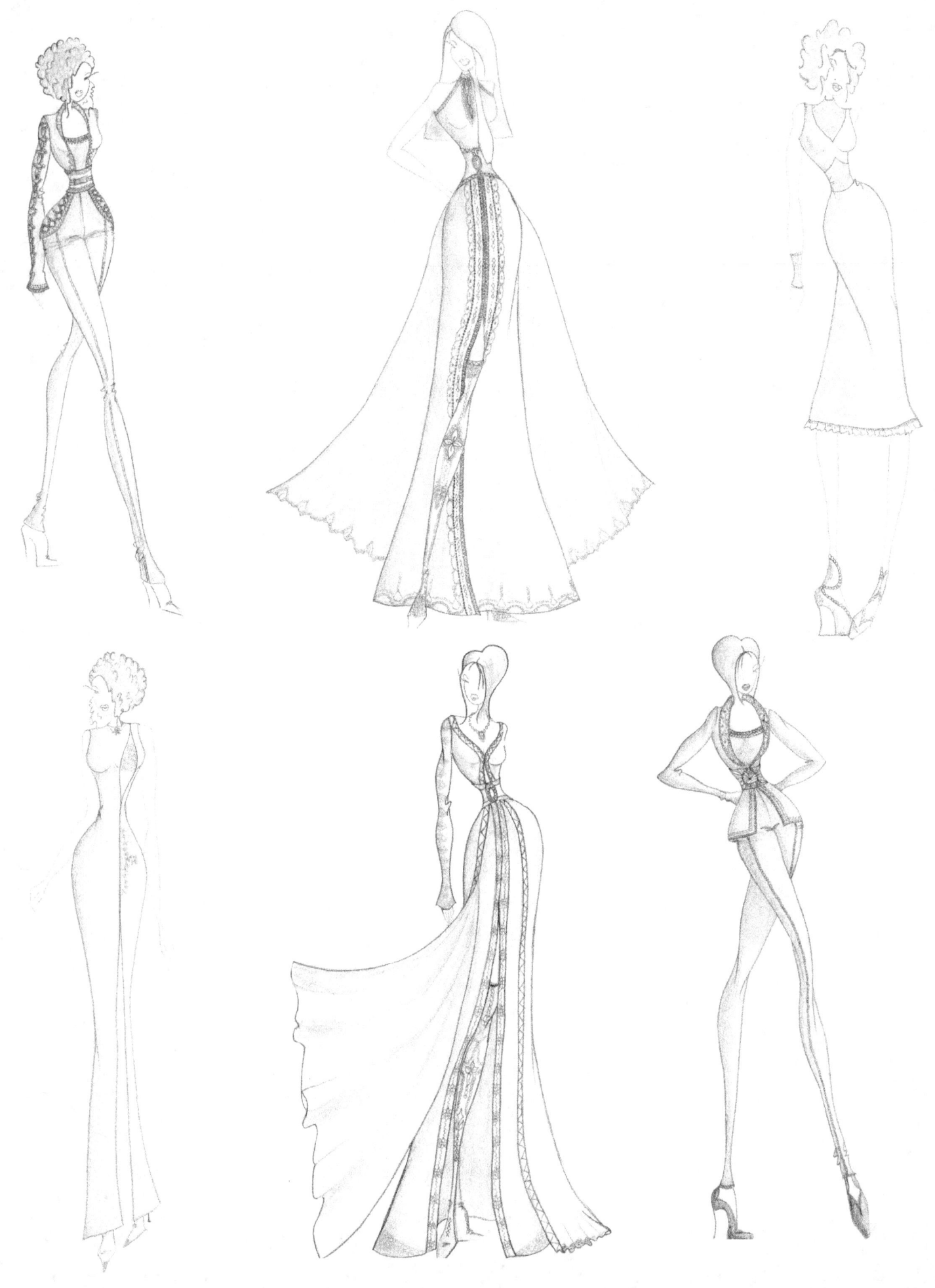

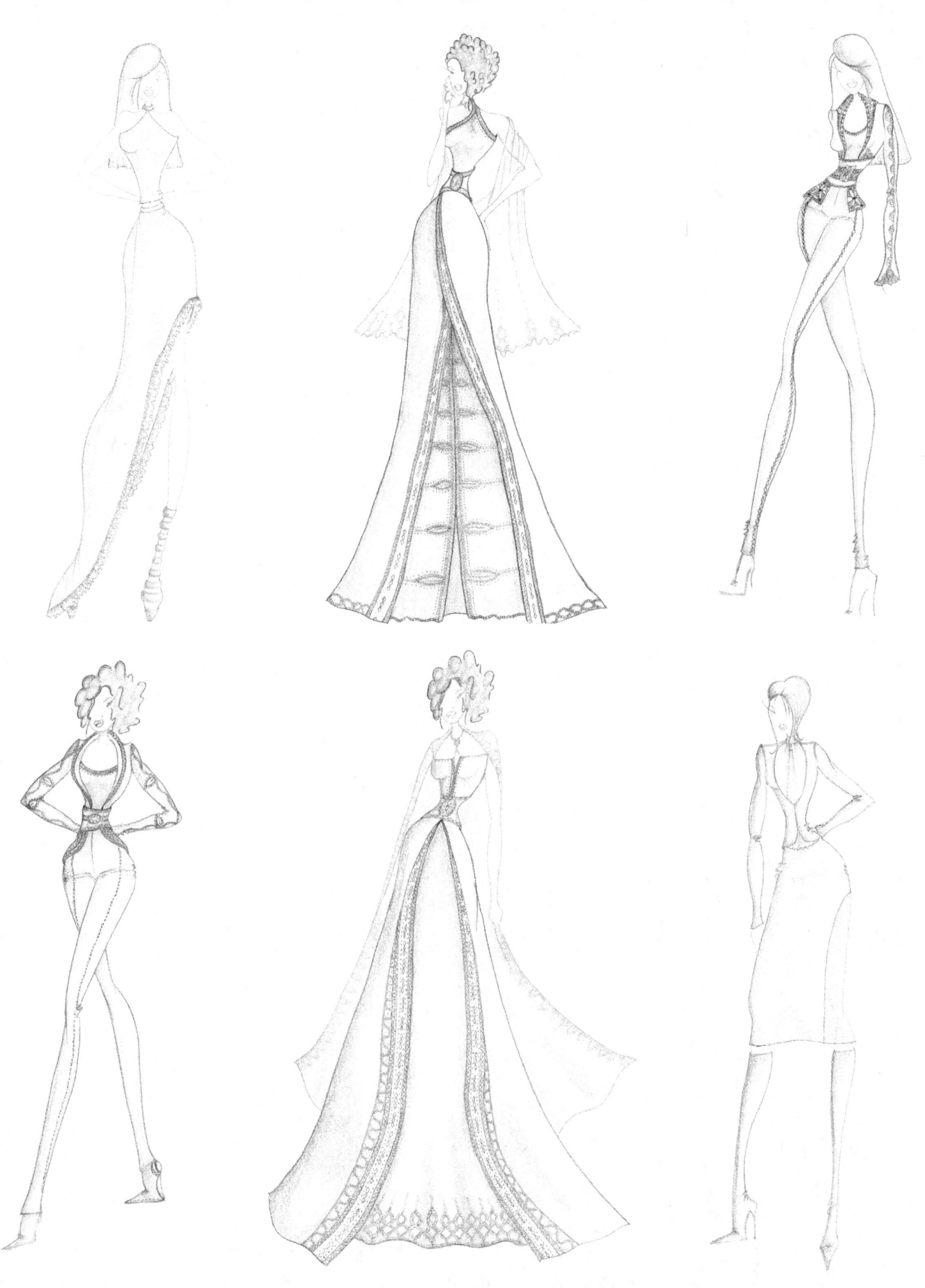

Fatima Al-Fihiri

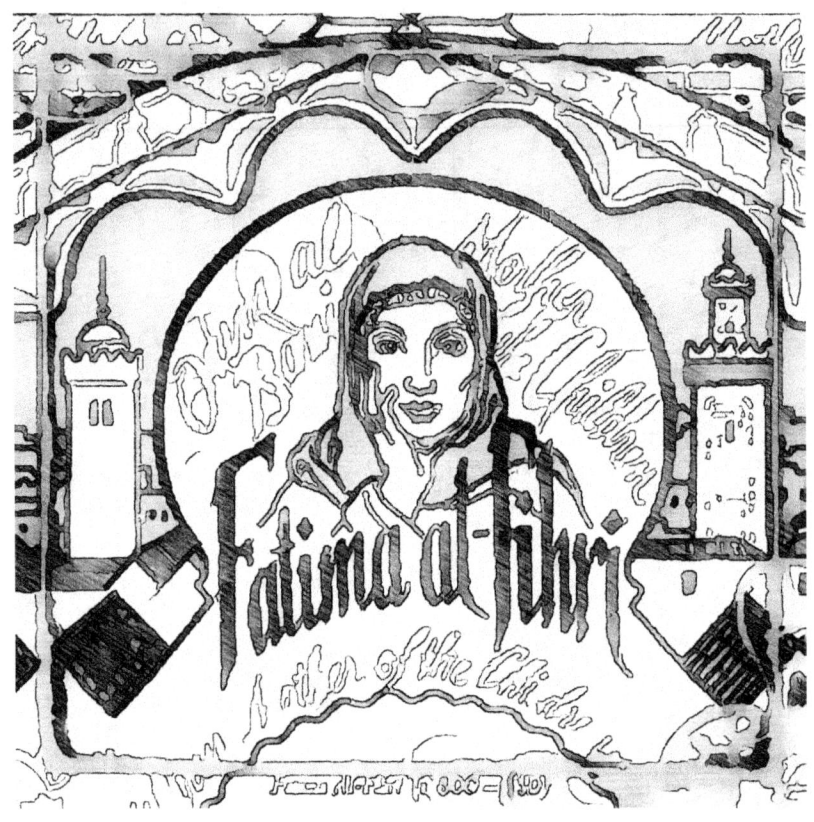

Fatima Al-Fihri, a young woman who was fascinated with knowledge, she laid the groundwork for a complex that would include a library, a mosque and a university. The university that Fatima Al-Fihri helped to found, she also attended and the library still holds her original diploma, back then on a wooden board not paper.

Muhammad Ibn Abd El-Karim El-Khattabi

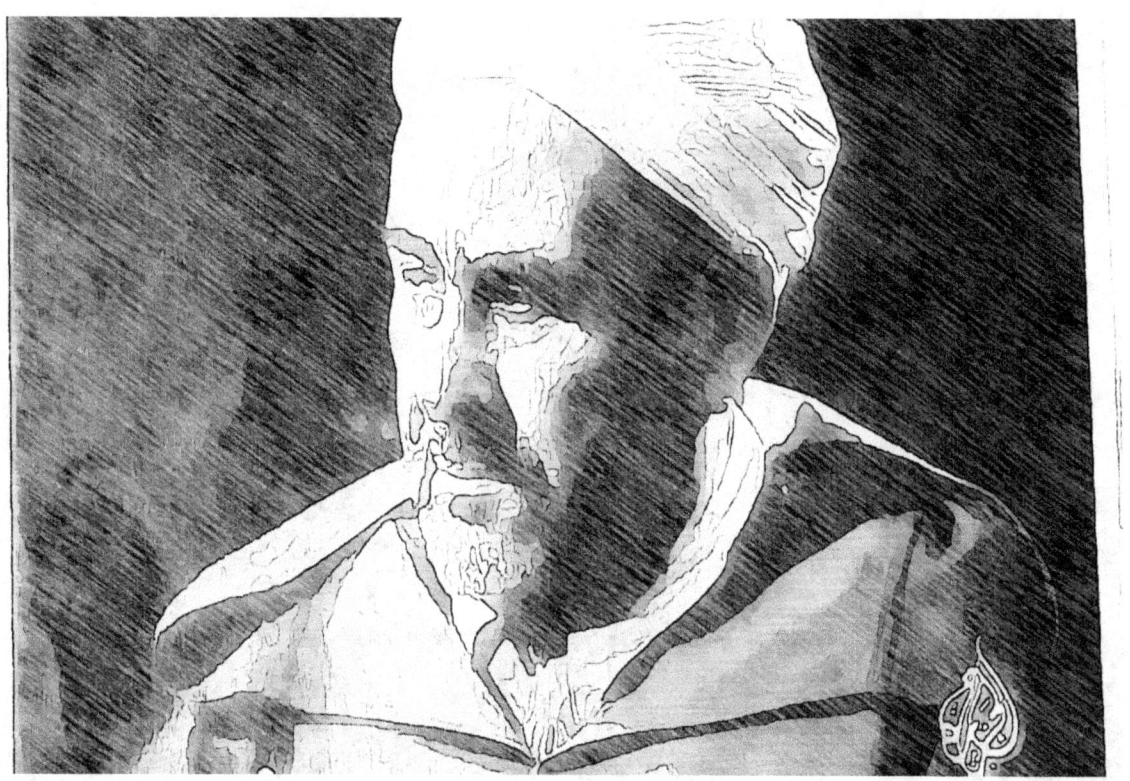

A very successful leader of resistance against foreign rule of the people in northern Morocco. Born in 1882 in Ajdir in the Rif region in northern Morocco, Mohammed Ben Abd El-Karim El-Khattabi also know as Abdelkrim fiercely resisted Spanish colonialism. He had a traditional education finishing at the Qarawine University in Fez 1906. Then he moved to Melilla a Spanish enclave in northern Morocco. He worked as a teacher and translator been as he was fluent in Spanish and Riffian. He worked for the Spanish 'native affairs' office and became a journalist for the Spanish newspaper and went on to become secretary-interpreter in the Native Affairs Office in Melilla, gaining a good reputation for discretion, efficiency and intelligence. He worked closely with the Spanish military bureaucracy until the end of World War I. This is when he, his father and brother found out about the real colonialist intention of Spanish rule over Morocco. During World War I, Abd el-Krim was arrested and imprisoned in Chaouen in 1916 by the Spanish authorities during World War I, for alleged involvement in a conspiracy with the German consul Dr. Walter Zechlin. In 1918 he escaped. In January 1919 he returned home to Ajdir and decided to fight for his tribe's independence, alarmed by the appearance of Spanish military in Ayt Weryaghel tribal territory. In 1920 together with his brother, Abd el-Krim began a war of rebellion against the Spanish. He wanted to unite the tribes of the Rif into an independent Republic to dismantle the French-Spanish colonial plan in Morocco. Spanish troops occupied areas of the Rif and Abd-el-Krim sent the General Manuel Fernández Silvestre a warning not to cross the Ameqqran river otherwise he would consider it an act of war.

Muhammad Ibn Abd El-Karim El-Khattabi

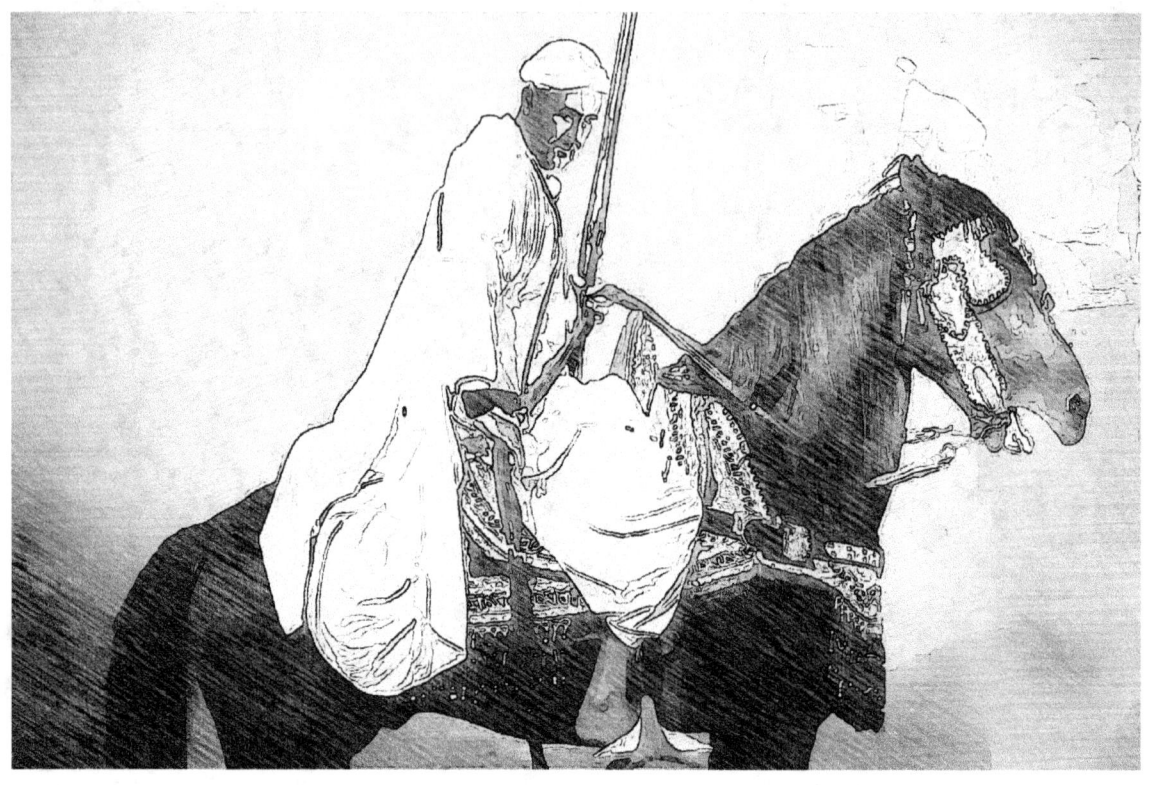

Not taking the warning seriously, Silvestre crossed the river and set up a military camp of 60,000 men. In June 1921 a Riffian force attacked, Abd el-Krim then directed his forces to attack the Spanish lines at Anwal, with great success. General Silvestre committed suicide after seeing his soldiers defeated. The Rifians' victory established Abd el-Krim as a master of guerrilla warfare and the president of the Republic of the Rif. Defeated by an army of 30,000 Rifian fighters the remainder of the 60,000 Spanish soldiers fled to the coast and into Melilla. The embarrassing defeat of the Spanish troops caused political commotion in Spain. After Abd el-Krim invaded French-occupied Morocco in April 1925 the French decided to take strong action and sent a massive 250,000+ soldiers combined with the Spanish army to Morocco. Intense combat lasted ten months, the combined French and Spanish armies using chemical bombs against the population caused Abd el-Krim to surrender to the French on May 26, 1926. He was exiled to French territory in the Indian Ocean from 1926 to 1947. He continued to push to keep western trends from imposing on Moroccan culture. In 1947 he was granted permission to live in the south of France. However, he was successful in gaining asylum in Egypt instead, by taking advantage of a stopover of his ship in Port Said in Egypt, where he managed to flee. After Morocco gained independence he was invited back to Morocco but he refused as long as French forces were on North African soil. He died in Egypt on February 6, 1963.

Morocco's Textiles

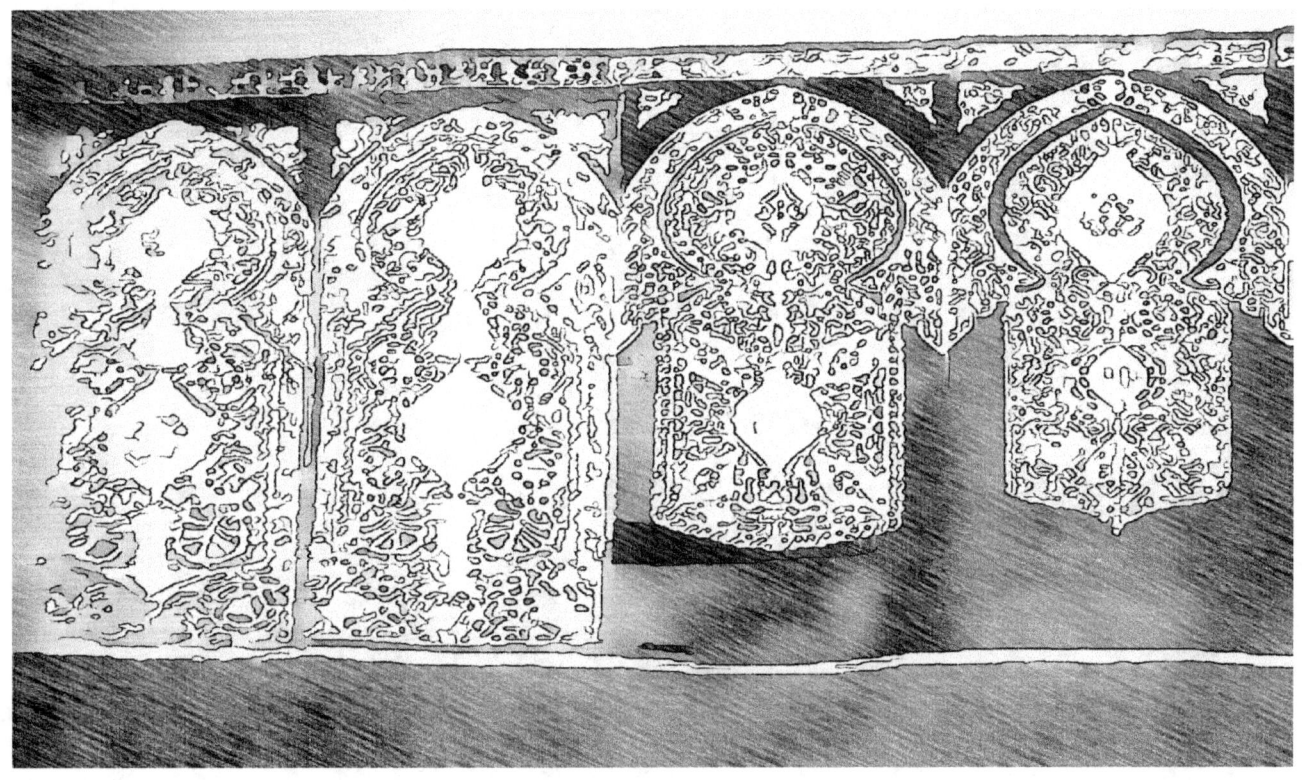

The heritage of textile production in Morocco is long reaching and dates way back to around 1500 BC when Berbers first came to North Africa bringing with them fundamental weaving and embroidery techniques that have been preserved over the centuries. At later dates strongly influenced by the Islamic Arab culture and after by the Jewish and European techniques. But what really distinguishes Moroccan textiles is the embroidery. In accordance with the architecture, intricate with elaborate ornamentation and repetitive geometric shapes which are sewn into the cloth individually.

The textiles are used in ceremonies such weddings, funerals and as gifts worn and carried to tombs to honor saints. Moroccan tribal textiles with vibrant colours, pattern variations and a variety of textures, are some of the most impressive and dazzling in Africa. They are distinctive to Morocco.

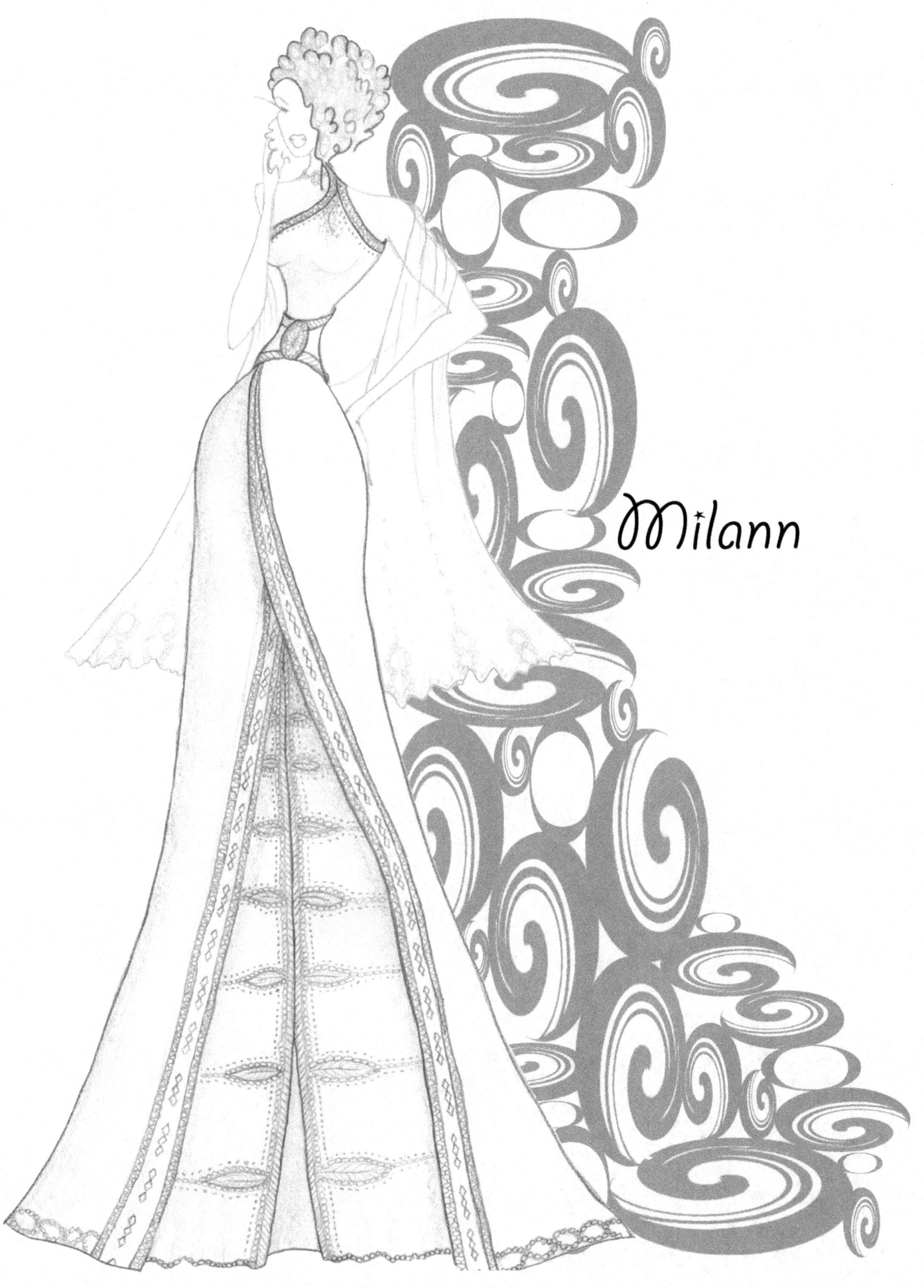

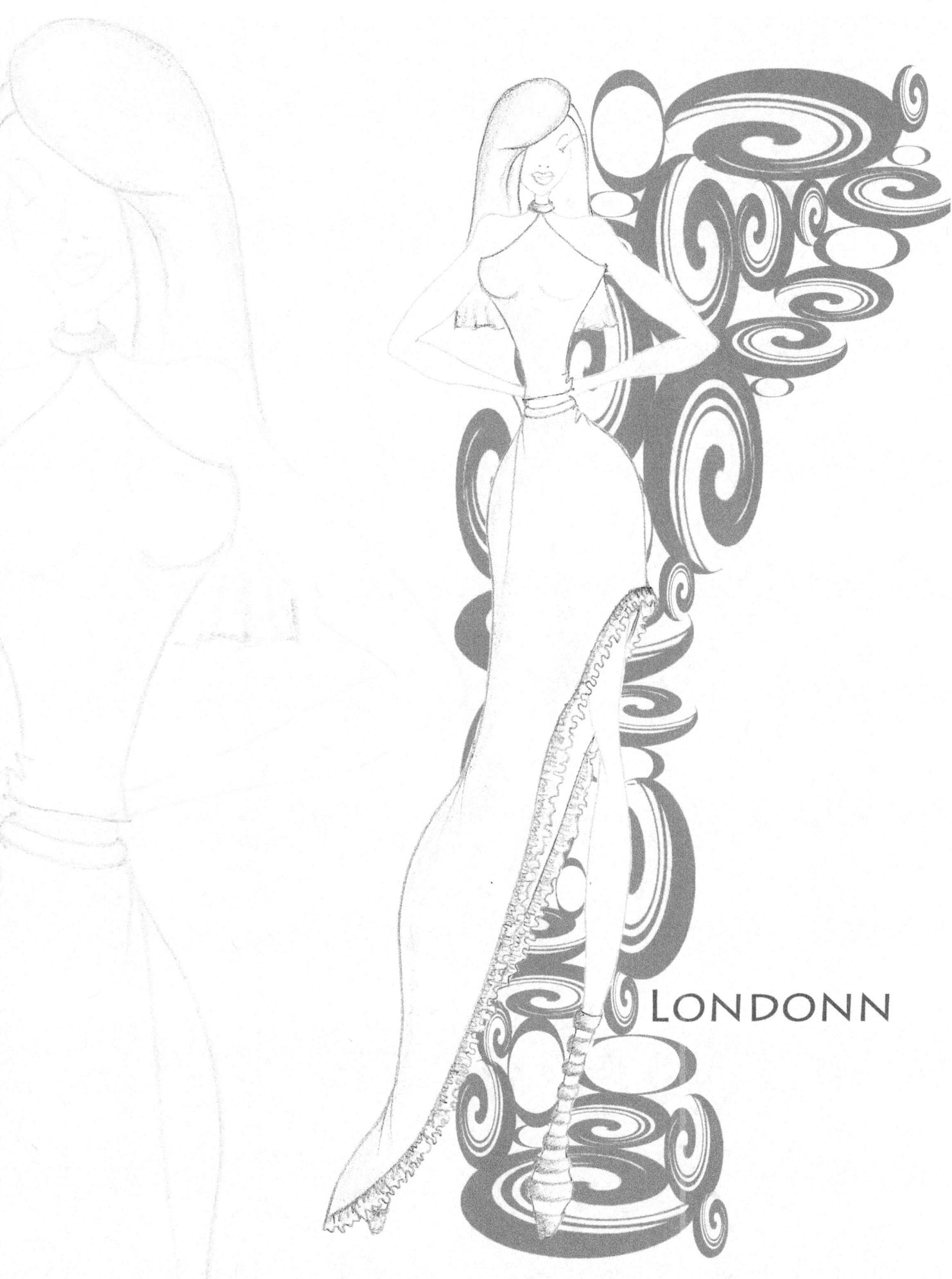

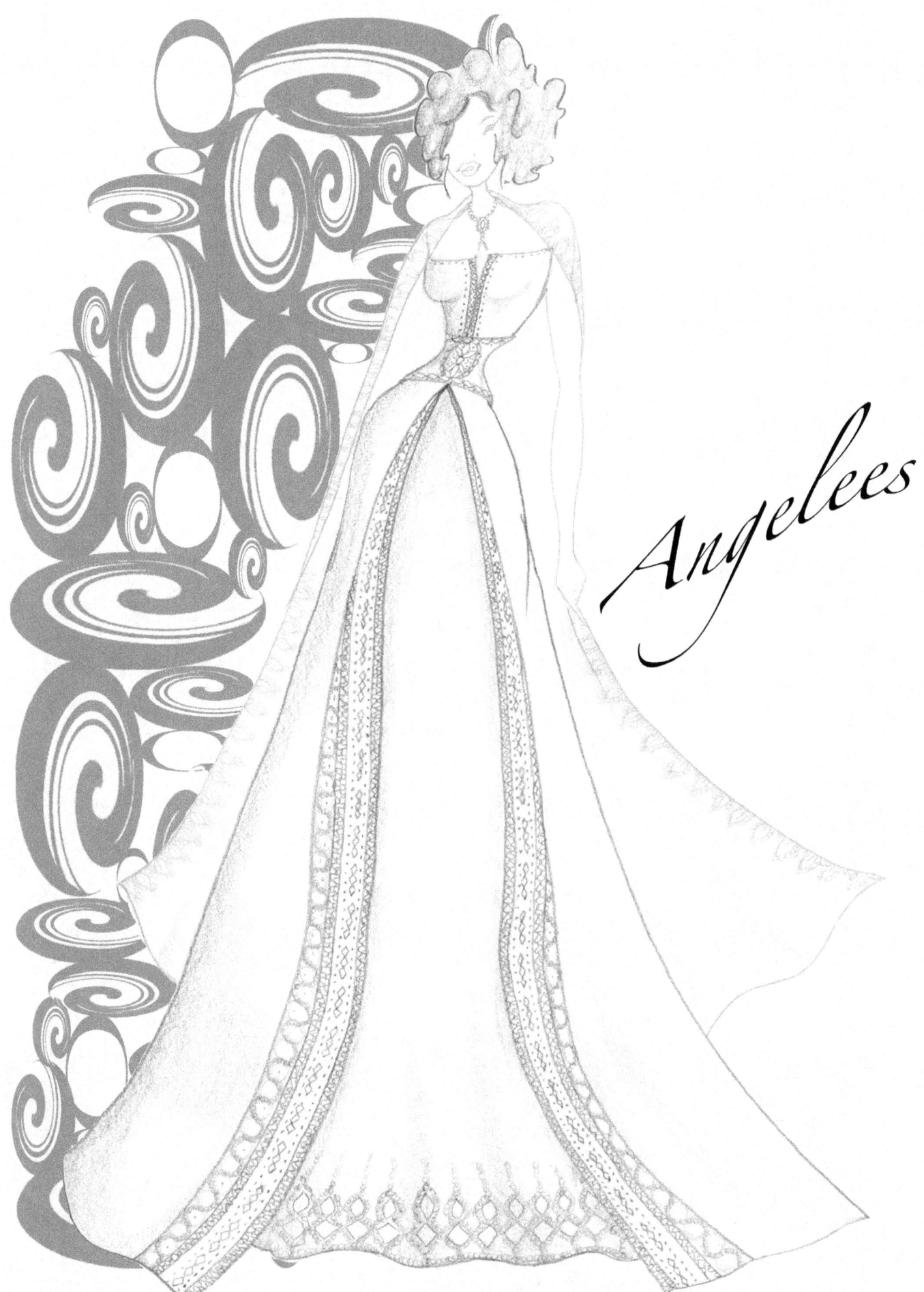

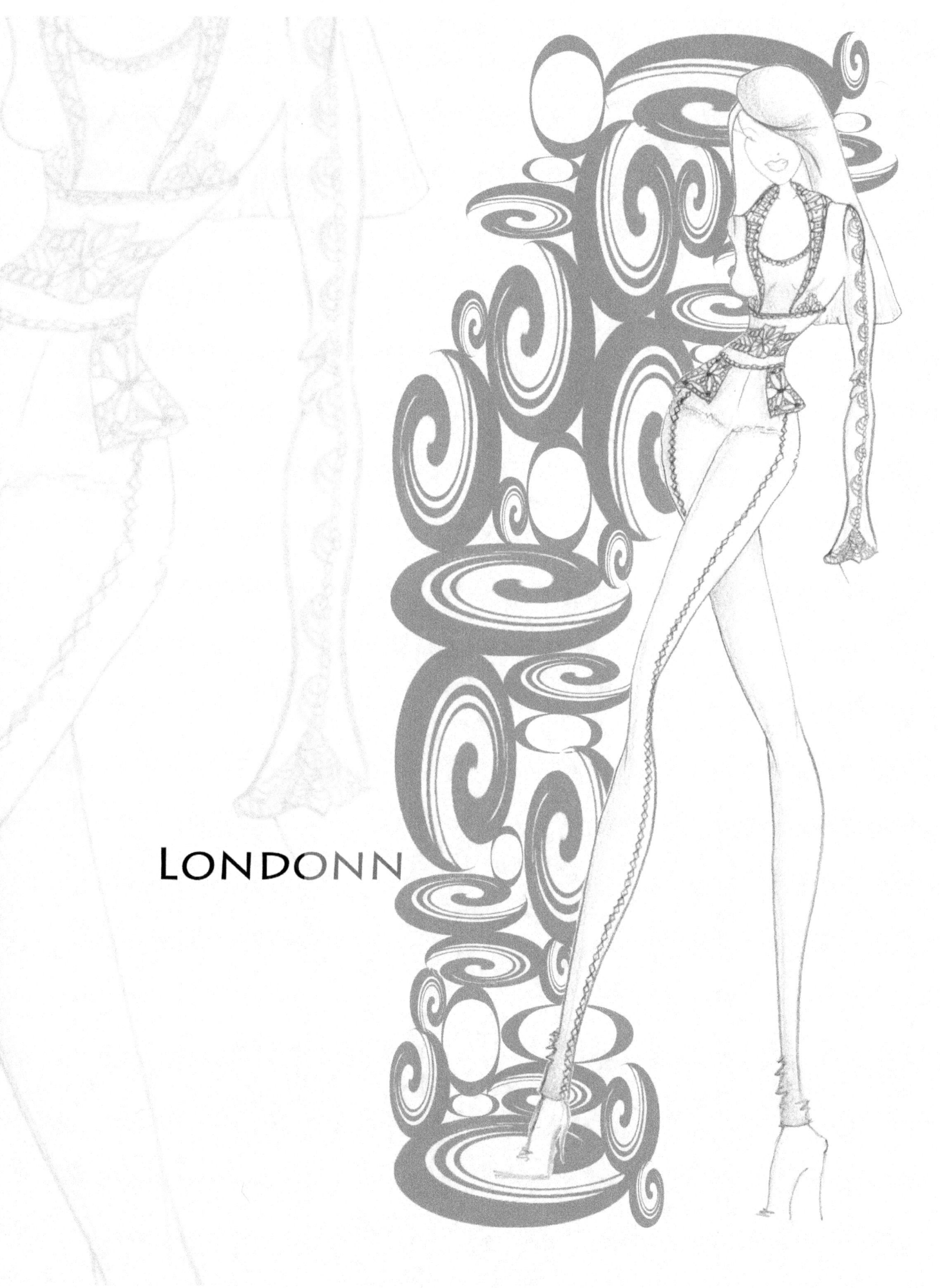

LONDONN

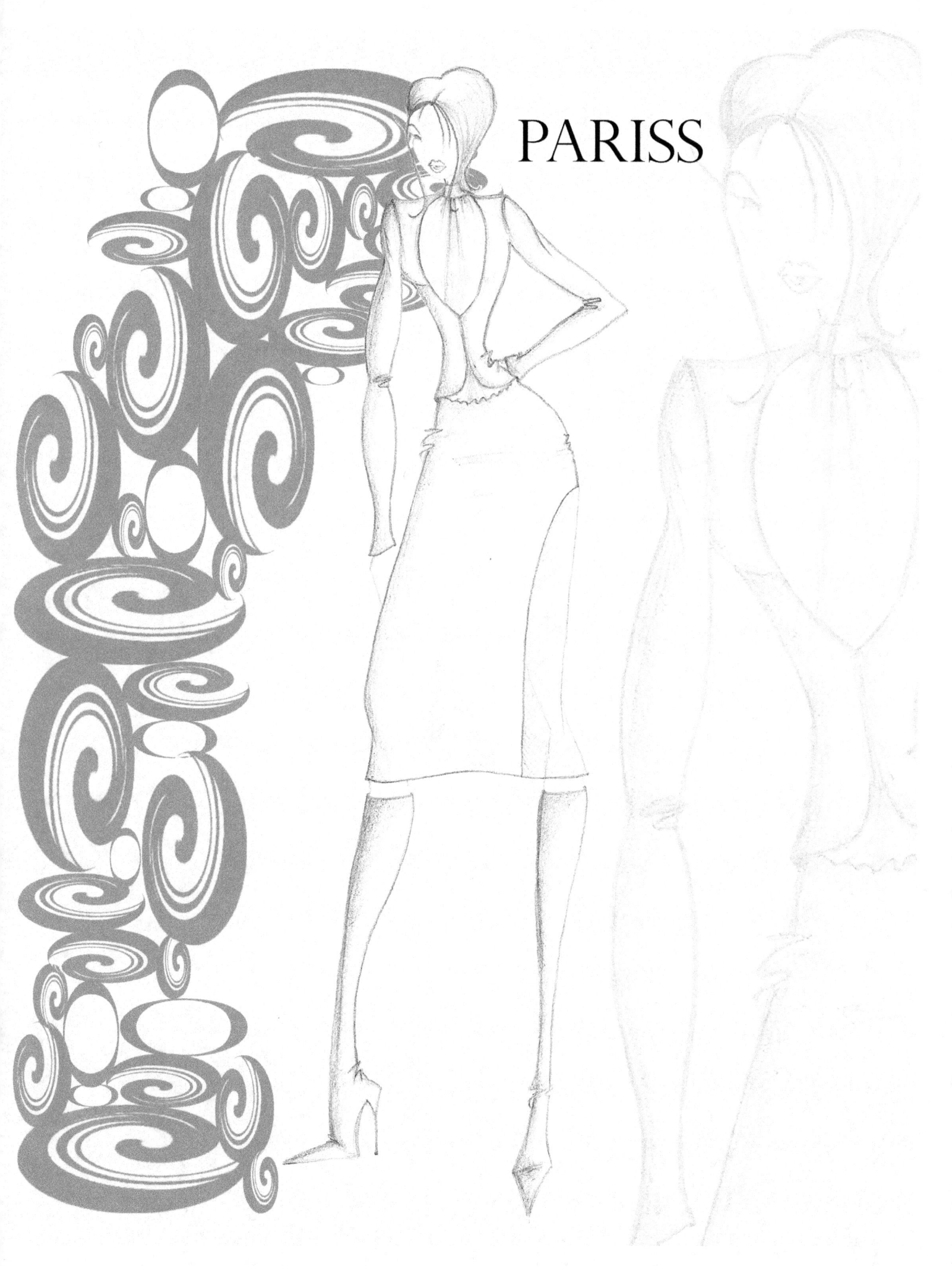

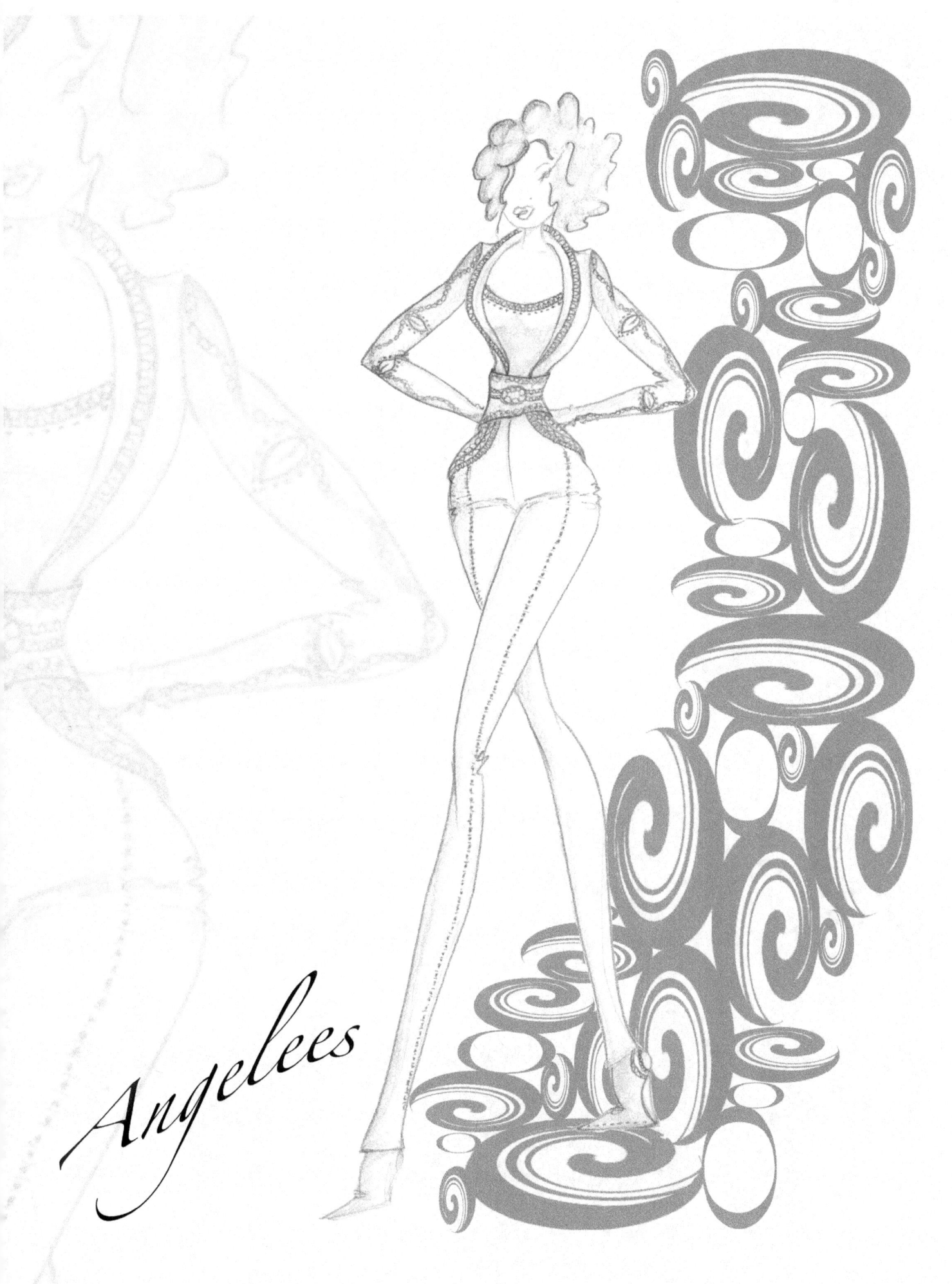

www.ingramcontent.com/pod-product-compliance
Lightning Source LLC
Chambersburg PA
CBHW062344220526
45469CB00008B/2836